Seeking God

PETER JEFFERY

BRYNTIRION Press
Wales, UK

Solid Ground Christian Books
Vestavia Hills, AL, USA

Published by:

BRYNTIRION Press
Bryntirion, Bridgend CF31 4DX
Wales, United Kingdom

and

Solid Ground Christian Books
PO Box 660132
Vestavia Hills, AL 35266
205-443-0311

Previously published as ISBN: 1 85049 131 3

ISBN: 1 85049 190 9

First booklet edition in June 2002

Printed in the USA

1. SEEKING GOD

Do you want to know God? Are you really seeking him? Then let us make it clear from the outset that you will only find God through Jesus Christ. He said, 'I am the way and the truth and the life. No one comes to the Father except through me' (John 14:6).

It is not enough, however, for you to say, 'I am seeking God.' What are your reasons for doing so?

Curiosity

Do not confuse seeking with being curious. The person who is only curious about God and spiritual things will never find the Lord. His search will easily and frequently be diverted to other things. His desire for God soon passes. Curiosity such as this can arise simply because it is in the person's nature to show a casual and temporary interest in various matters. Or it could be that a friend has been genuinely converted, and curiosity is aroused as to what has caused the change in him. This latter cause is often used by the Holy Spirit to produce a genuine seeking.

Intellectual enquiry

There are some people who delight to describe themselves as seekers after truth. Such seeking is not a true seeking after God, but an intellectual exercise that never brings satisfaction. This 'seeker' may be genuine, sincere and earnest, but he is never desperate. His need is intellectual, not spiritual; he is seeking not God, but knowledge. We will be showing later that the mind *is* important in coming to true faith in God. God speaks to a man *through* the mind and *to* the heart. The Christian does not despise the intellect, but he recognizes its limitations.

Peace of mind

There are also those who seek God as an answer to their marriage, family or other emotional problems. They turn to God as they would turn to an aspirin when they have a headache. With these people there is no

1

consciousness of personal sin. God is merely a way of escape. What they are looking for is not a Savior but an emotional crutch. One can have more sympathy with these folk than with the curious or intellectual seekers; but still they will not find God, for there is a vast difference between peace of mind and peace with God.

Deep longing

This is the way to seek God. 'You will seek me and find me when you seek me with all your heart' (Jeremiah 29:13). The person who is truly seeking God is doing so because he has been made aware of the state of his soul. He knows that he is a sinner. Do you object to being called a sinner? The true seeker does not. In the eyes of society he may be considered the height of respectability, but in the sight of God, he knows he is vile and full of sin. So he seeks God not out of curiosity, not because of intellectual interest, nor merely as a remedy for instability, but because of a deep and desperate need for pardon and forgiveness.

The difference between this man and the other three is that he can truly see his problem. He may or may not be curious by nature. He may be an intellectual or quite the opposite. He may have a life full of emotional instability or be devoid of any such problems. But whatever else is true of him, he knows that he is a sinner, and there is a longing in his soul to be right with God. This difference between him and others has nothing to do with temperament, ability or background. It is the emerging evidence of the Holy Spirit working in his life. He is going through a painful experience, but by the grace of God it will lead him to salvation through Jesus Christ.

It is for such a person that this little book is written. The curious seeker will not benefit from it; in all probability he will not read it all the way through, but will lose interest very soon. The intellectual seeker will argue with everything and will find no satisfaction in these pages. To both of these I would say very solemnly that there is no virtue in merely seeking. You will seek your way to hell, unless you see that your real need is to seek a Savior. The 'peace-of-mind' seeker could benefit, if he comes to see that his real problem is that he needs a Savior. He must reach the point where he recognizes that even if he had no emotional problems of any kind, he still has a problem of sin, and this problem can only be answered in the Lord Jesus Christ.

For the person who has a deep longing for peace with God, it is my prayer that these pages may be a stepping stone to a living faith in the Lord Jesus Christ.

> Seek the Lord while he may be found; call on him while he is near.
> Let the wicked forsake his way and the evil man his thoughts.
> Let him turn to the Lord, and he will have mercy on him,
> and to our God, for he will freely pardon (Isaiah 55:6,7).

The benefits and blessings of being a Christian

'If I become a Christian, I will have to give up many of my pleasures.' This sort of thinking is often in the mind of the person seeking God. But the truth is that no one ever gives up anything for God without receiving much more in return. The person who thinks in this way is like a man who has hobbled about with a crippling disease for many years complaining, 'If I am healed, I will have to give up my crutches.'

Simon Peter once said to Jesus, 'We have left everything to follow you!' 'I tell you the truth', Jesus replied, 'no one who has left home or brothers or sisters or mother or father or children or fields for me and the gospel will fail to receive a hundred times as much in the present age ...and in the age to come, eternal life' (Mark 10:28-30).

This truth is confirmed in the experience of the apostle Paul, as he says in Philippians 3:7,8: 'But whatever was to my profit I now consider loss for the sake of Christ. What is more, I consider everything a loss compared to the surpassing greatness of knowing Christ Jesus my Lord, for whose sake I have lost all things. I consider them rubbish, that I may gain Christ.'

Before he was converted, Paul (or Saul of Tarsus, as he was then known) was a young man with enormous prospects. His pedigree was faultless (see Philippians 3:5,6). It is obvious from Acts 7:58 and 9:1,2 that he was already a leader in his own circle. But when he was converted, all this changed, and instead he knew extreme hardship and much danger. Read

2 Corinthians 11:23-28. Many would say, 'What a waste!' But that is not what Paul says: he speaks rather of 'the surpassing greatness of knowing Christ Jesus'. What a beautiful phrase that is! You probably cannot understand it at the moment, but if you are really seeking God it may not be too long before this will also be your testimony.

There is nothing to be compared with the joy of knowing the Lord Jesus Christ as your Savior. The difficulties and problems of the Christian life are very real, but the benefits and blessings far outweigh them.

Consider some of the benefits to the Christian: sins forgiven (1 John 1:9); peace with God (Romans 5:1); a new life (2 Corinthians 5:17); and heaven guaranteed (John 14:1-3). And so we could go on; the list is endless. To become a Christian is the greatest thing that can happen to you.

In the 19th century there was a very famous scientist in Scotland by the name of Sir James Simpson. He made many valuable medical discoveries, among them the use of chloroform as the first anaesthetic. But when asked at a public meeting what his greatest discovery had been, this remarkable man replied without hesitation: 'That I have a Savior.'

The same man said, 'In Christ you will find a Savior, a companion, a counselor, a friend, a brother who loves you with a love greater than the human heart can conceive.'

2. SIN

Why do you have to seek God? Why is it so difficult to do so? Why don't all men know and love God? The answer to all these questions is: SIN.

> Your iniquities have separated you from your God; your sins
> have hidden his face from you, so that he will not hear (Isaiah 59:2).

> For all have sinned and fall short of the glory of God (Romans 3:23).

Sin is a very real problem. It has always been the major problem facing society, and thousands of years of history and scientific progress have not changed the situation. It is man's selfishness and greed that cause many to be hungry, produce broken homes and create a drug problem. Every known social problem can be traced back to the fact that man in his sin has rejected God's way. Man may be a stone-age sinner or a twenty-first-century space-age sinner, but sinner he is, and sin never produces anything but misery.

But sin is not just the problem of society; it is also the problem of the individual. It is *your* problem. *You* are a sinner.

If you are truly seeking God, it is because you have become aware of your own sin and guilt. You know it is a problem. You may have tried to reform your life, but even if to some degree you have succeeded, the fact of sin still makes God a stranger to you.

This is a problem too big for you or any human being to overcome. We shall see in the next few pages why this is so, and we shall also see that God is able to deal with sin.

Sin's origin

Man was made in the image of God. This does not mean a physical resemblance, but speaks of a capacity given to man at creation so that he could know and enjoy God. Man was created in righteousness, and it was his privilege to enjoy fellowship and communion with God.

This fellowship was shattered by what is commonly called 'the fall of man'. The events are related in the third chapter of Genesis. The story of Adam and Eve is generally regarded as a myth today. That is a tragic mistake, for the events recorded in that chapter have more bearing on your life today than anything that is currently happening. It is here that we have the origin of sin in man's nature.

God is holy. There is no sin in him. He cannot sin. God cannot lie, cheat, envy, or sin in any way. But more than that: not only is he not evil; he is righteous and just. God is light, and in him there is no darkness at all. He dwells in the realm of light. His holiness is a consuming fire. It follows, then, that everything God does or produces will be good. The world that God created, and everything in it, including man, was good. Sin was no part of creation; it is an intrusion into God's world, inspired by the devil.

5

The holy God gave man righteous and just laws by which to live a full and happy life. But sin is a rejection of God's character and authority; it is an attack on the holiness of God. 'Everyone who sins breaks the law; in fact, sin is lawlessness' (1 John 3:4).

This is clearly illustrated in Genesis 3. We read in Genesis 2:17 of the one restriction which God put upon man in the paradise of Eden: 'You must not eat from the tree of the knowledge of good and evil, for when you eat of it you will surely die.' That is the clear command and warning given by God. The devil comes to Eve in the form of a serpent, and his first approach is to cast doubt on the command: 'Did God really say?' (3:1). Then he contradicts the warning: 'You will not surely die' (3:4). Finally, he openly attacks the goodness of God (3:5) by suggesting that God has imposed this restriction because he is afraid that Adam and Eve will become like him, and then he will have rivals.

Adam and Eve are deceived. They disobey God, and sin becomes part of man's nature: 'Sin entered the world through one man, and death through sin, and in this way death came to all men, because all sinned' (Romans 5:12). In other words, it became part of our human nature—that nature that we have all inherited from Adam—to rebel against God. But more than that: the serious consequences of such rebellion—what the apostle Paul calls 'death through sin'—also became part of our experience. It is desperately important that we should understand what this means.

Sin's consequences

The consequences of the entering in of sin into man's nature are enormous. Here are some of them:

Lost privileges

When sin entered in, man lost many precious privileges.

He lost *peace with God*. 'I was afraid ...so I hid' (Genesis 3:10). Men are still afraid of God and are still hiding from him. Many try to camouflage this by denying that God exists.

He lost *access to God*. Sin bars us from the holy presence of God. Genesis chapter 3 ends with man being driven from Eden. This is what the

Scriptures mean when they say that man is spiritually dead: he is without God in the world. And nothing has changed; the holy God will no more tolerate sin in us than he did in Adam. Of heaven he says, 'Nothing impure will ever enter it, nor will anyone who does what is shameful or deceitful' (Revelation 21:27).

He lost *eternal life*. We have already seen that God warned Adam that if he sinned he would die (Genesis 2:17). Adam did sin, and immediately he knew spiritual death; he died to God. This was later followed by physical death. Similarly if you are not a Christian, you are spiritually dead; your soul is dead; it can make no response to God. And one day your body will die. Why? A doctor will put on your death certificate that the cause of death is cancer, or a heart attack, or pneumonia, or some such disease. But he will be wrong. These sicknesses are merely the *means* of death. The *cause* of death is sin. You will die because you are a sinner: 'The wages of sin is death' (Romans 6:23).

A polluted nature

Another of the terrible effects of the entering in of sin is that it pollutes every part of man's nature.

Sin affects our *minds*. 'The sinful mind is hostile to God. It does not submit to God's law, nor can it do so' (Romans 8:7). 'The man without the Spirit does not accept the things that come from the Spirit of God, for they are foolishness to him and he cannot understand them' (1 Corinthians 2:14).

Sin also affects our *freedom*. 'Everyone who sins is a slave to sin' (John 8:34).

And sin affects our *desires*. 'All of us also lived ...at one time, gratifying the cravings of our sinful nature and following its desires and thoughts' (Ephesians 2:3).

This is not a pretty picture, but it is an accurate description of the effects of sin upon human nature. Before we go on to mention the other consequences of sin, pause for a moment to consider what we have said already.

Perhaps you are the type of person who, quite rightly, hates to hear of injustice and suffering. The sort of suffering we have seen in recent years in countries torn by war may fill you with horror. Can you not see that this is the product of man's sin—that same sin that causes *you* to envy, or lose your temper, or gossip? The New Testament says of men who are without God that 'They are full of envy, murder, strife, deceit and malice. They are gossips, slanderers, God-haters, insolent, arrogant and boastful; they invent ways of doing evil; they disobey their parents; they are senseless, faithless, heartless, ruthless' (Romans 1:29-31). Many of the sins in this list may not be true of you; but some of them are, and they all come from the same seed-bed of rebellion against God. You are seeking God because you are becoming aware of the awful effect of sin in your own life. That is good. At the moment you may not have an answer to sin, but at least you are not blind to it.

The wrath of God

But the entry of sin has even worse consequences than those we have mentioned. Not only does sin make man a stranger to God, an enemy of God, 'dead in ...transgressions and sins' (Ephesians 2:1). But sin puts him under the wrath of God.

Make no mistake about it: God is angry with sin. 'The wrath of God is being revealed from heaven against all the godlessness and wickedness of men' (Romans 1:18). Worse still, men are 'by nature objects of [God's] wrath' (Ephesians 2:3).

Judgment

The consequences of sin do not end with death. 'It is appointed unto men once to die, but after this the judgment' (Hebrews 9:27 AV). All men are answerable to Almighty God and will one day stand before him to give an account. Read what Jesus says of this day of judgment in Matthew 25:31-46.

Hell

Do you believe in hell? It is obvious from Matthew 25 that Jesus did. Listen to some of the things the Son of God said about this place which

God has prepared for unrepentant sinners: 'The Son of Man will send out his angels, and they will weed out of his kingdom everything that causes sin and all who do evil. They will throw them into the fiery furnace, where there will be weeping and gnashing of teeth' (Matthew 13:41,42). Again, in Mark 9:43, he describes it as 'hell, where the fire never goes out'. This is terrible, but it is the just and deserved reward for sin. That is why you need to seek God for pardon and forgiveness.

3. THE REMEDY FOR SIN

People resent being told that they are sinners. They will admit that they are not perfect, but think they are not too bad really—as good as most people, they like to believe, and better than some. The tendency therefore is to treat sin and its consequences lightly, and it is an easy step from there for man to think that he can provide his own remedy for sin.

Man's remedy

Here are some of the remedies people argue for:

Good works

Try your best, say some. Be kind. Be helpful. Be interested in some charity and work hard for it. This is the way to be sure of heaven.

Morality

For others the answer is: be honest and true. Do not lie or cheat. Do not be immoral in any way. Surely God cannot expect more than that of any man!

But what does God's Word say about good works and morality as a remedy for sin and a means of salvation? 'All our righteous acts are like filthy rags' (Isaiah 64:6). 'For it is by grace that you have been saved, through faith ...not by works, so that no one can boast' (Ephesians 2:8).

Good works and morality are to be commended, but they cannot put sin right. They cannot take away God's anger and they cannot save your soul. 'He saved us, not because of righteous things we had done, but because of his mercy' (Titus 3:5).

Religion

According to others the remedy for sin must surely lie in religion. Go to church. Be faithful and devout. Say your prayers.

Once again, these things are good and highly commendable, but they are only another form of good works and morality. The problem of sin remains unanswered. Read the story in Mark 10:17-27 of the man who was good, moral and religious, but had no salvation and no eternal life.

There are many people who believe in all sincerity that their remedies for sin are good enough, and that these things will most surely earn them a place in heaven.

Think of a great sporting event that takes place each year. The demand for tickets to see this event is enormous, and every year we hear of counterfeit tickets being sold. These are very much like the official tickets, but they are false; they do not carry the authority of the sports governing body. It is easy to imagine an avid fan buying one of these counterfeit tickets, believing it to be genuine and that it guarantees him a seat for the big match. With great expectation he travels hundreds of miles to the stadium, only to be turned away at the gate. His sincerity, and his belief that the ticket was genuine, are of no avail at all. He has been deceived. There is no entrance for him.

Satan is the great deceiver. He is an expert at producing counterfeit ways of salvation. Be careful. Be sure that your hope rests in the way God himself has prepared for sinners. It is God's remedy for sin that you need, not your own.

God's remedy

'For God so loved the world that he gave his one and only Son, that whoever believes in him shall not perish but have eternal life' (John 3:16). Here we have a perfect statement of God's glorious remedy for sin.

God hates sin, but in his divine love he has prepared a remedy which deals justly with the punishment that sin deserves, and yet at the same time provides pardon for the sinner.

God has said that the penalty for sin is death—spiritual and physical death. Nothing can change that, because it is the judgment of the holy God. As such it is perfect and correct. God will not pretend that a man has not sinned. Justice must be done. The demands of God's law and the penalties for breaking that law must be satisfied.

In love and mercy God declares that he will accept a substitute to die in the sinner's place. But God's law demands the substitute must be free from the guilt of sin, and therefore not deserving of death himself.

There was no man who met these requirements. So God became man— a holy, perfect, sinless man, whose name was Jesus. Read very carefully the following words from Romans 3:25,26: 'God presented him as a sacrifice of atonement, through faith in his blood. He did this to demonstrate his justice, because in his forbearance he had left the sins committed beforehand unpunished—he did it to demonstrate his justice at the present time, so as to be just and the one who justifies the man who has faith in Jesus.'

Now turn to Ephesians 2 and read that chapter carefully. Here is God's remedy for your sin. It is all of grace. 'Grace' means that you did nothing to deserve such a remedy, and that you contributed nothing toward it. This should encourage you in seeking God. It is not that you seek God, but that God seeks you. The Lord God Almighty has himself provided a remedy for your sin so that you may know and love him. This remedy is to be found only in the Lord Jesus Christ. So, in seeking God, it is vital that you know who Jesus is.

4. JESUS CHRIST

Jesus is God. God reveals himself in Scripture as God the Father, God the Son, and God the Holy Spirit. This is called the Trinity. There are not three separate Gods, but one God. This is a great mystery: none the less it is a fact.

Jesus was not just a good man, a healer, a teacher, a prophet. He was all of those things. But he is the eternal Son of God. He is divine. 'In the beginning was the Word, and the Word was with God, and the Word was God' (John 1:1). The whole of the first chapter of John makes it clear that Jesus is 'the Word'. 'The Word became flesh and lived for a while among us' (verse 14).

The New Testament leaves us in no doubt as to who Jesus is. 'He is the image of the invisible God, the firstborn over all creation. For by him all things were created' (Colossians 1:15, 16). 'For God was pleased to have all his fulness dwell in him' (Colossians 1:19). 'For in Christ all the fulness of the Deity lives in bodily form' (Colossians 2:9). 'The Son is the radiance of God's glory and the exact representation of his being' (Hebrews 1:3).

In the Old Testament the prophet Isaiah was given a remarkable revelation of the glory and holiness of God. He sees and hears the angelic host crying, 'Holy, holy, holy is the Lord Almighty; the whole earth is full of his glory' (Isaiah 6:3). The prophet himself says, 'My eyes have seen the King, the Lord Almighty' (verse 5). In the New Testament the apostle John refers to this incident and says, 'Isaiah said this because he saw Jesus' glory and spoke about him' (John 12:41).

Jesus is the holy God the angels spoke of. Jesus is the King, the Lord Almighty, whom Isaiah saw. Jesus is God.

The incarnation and life of Jesus

'Incarnation' comes from a Latin word meaning 'in the flesh' and refers to the birth of Jesus when God became man.

We have seen something of the problem of sin. It separates man from God and brings the wrath and judgment of the holy God upon us. There is nothing that man can do about this. But God in his great love and mercy can do something, and he does. He plans man's salvation.

This great plan is worked out in heaven in the mind and heart of God. It rests primarily upon an act of atonement being made on the sinner's behalf. The word 'atonement' literally means 'a making at one', and refers to the task of bringing sinners into a right relationship with God.

But who is to make the atonement? There is no man capable of it. All are in the same position; all deserve judgment and death. There is only one way: God becomes man. The Holy One identifies himself with sinful man; he takes our nature upon him. At Bethlehem this most amazing thing takes place. The hymn-writer, Charles Wesley, described it as

> Our God contracted to a span,
> Incomprehensibly made man.

And Paul said, 'Christ Jesus ...being in very nature God ...made himself nothing, taking the very nature of a servant, being made in human likeness. And being found in appearance as a man, he humbled himself and became obedient to death—even death on a cross!' (Philippians 2:5-8).

God had revealed a little of this plan in the Old Testament. Seven hundred years before Jesus was born Isaiah had said, 'The virgin will be with child and will give birth to a son, and will call him Immanuel' (Isaiah 7:14). The prophet Micah had said that the birth would take place in Bethlehem (Micah 5:2). The New Testament declares with great joy and ringing authority that Jesus is Immanuel. This is a Hebrew word meaning 'God with us' (See Matthew 1:18-25; Luke 1:26-38 and 2:1-20).

The birth of Jesus was very special. The Old Testament prophet Isaiah, and the New Testament writers Matthew and Luke all tell us that his mother Mary was a virgin. His birth was not the result of human love or lust, but the remarkable life-giving operation of the Holy Spirit (Matthew 1:20; Luke 1:35). This may be baffling to our minds, but it is vital to our salvation. If Jesus was the result of a normal sexual relationship between a man and woman, he would be like all men—a sinner by nature and helpless to save himself, let alone anyone else. Jesus did not inherit a sinful nature, and his life of obedience to the law of God kept his nature sinless and pure. In his life he was 'tempted in every way, just as we are—yet was without sin' (Hebrews 4:15).

This is of more than passing interest. It is crucial for our salvation. Jesus came to make atonement for our sin. That meant he had to die in our place, for that was the penalty God had decreed for sin. He came therefore to die as a sacrifice for us—to die in our stead. That was God's plan: 'He was pierced for our transgressions, he was crushed for our iniquities; the punishment that brought us peace was upon him, and by his wounds we are healed' (Isaiah 53:5).

But in order to do this Jesus had to be sinless, so that death should have no rightful claims on him. The slightest sin in Jesus would have made him no different from all other men, and would have been sufficient to bring upon him the penalty of death. He would then have to die for his own sins; in no way could he have offered to die instead of us. But, thank God, only hours before he was crucified, he was able to say, 'The prince of this world [the devil] is coming. He has no hold on me' (John 14:30). What Jesus was saying was that the devil had no claim upon him at all. The sinlessness of the Savior deprived the devil of any authority or control over him. More than that, it made it impossible for the Evil One to make any lawful demands upon Almighty God that the Lord Jesus Christ should die for his own sins.

5. CHRIST'S ATONING DEATH

Why is the death of Jesus Christ so crucial? The answer is that it is not his teaching, his parables, his miracles, his healings or his sinless life that saves us, but his atoning death.

You are a sinner, separated from God and under his holy wrath and judgment. Your religion, morality, or good works can do nothing to change the situation. Let us be clear about this. Your efforts, in and of themselves, are commendable and they help to make life better. But they cannot touch the real problem of sin.

Imagine a man driving down the highway in his car, and suddenly having trouble. After a few knocks and squeaks, the car comes to a halt at the side of the road. He gets out, knowing there is something wrong. What can it be? He wonders. After a brief inspection he sees that the windows are dirty. He gets out his little yellow duster and soon puts that right. But still the car will not start. Then he discovers that one of his tires is under-inflated, so out comes the foot pump and that fault is remedied. But that does not make the car go either!

Can you see what he is doing? He is dealing with problems, but he is avoiding the *real* problem. The trouble is that there is no power, no life in the engine; *that* is the thing which needs to be put right.

You may well be thinking that this is a silly illustration. No driver would be so stupid. Maybe not, but millions of people, in dealing with their souls, behave just like that. Religion, morality, and good works can deal only with minor problems. Man's real problem, a dead soul and a lifeless spirit, remains untouched. That is your condition *now*, and apart from the grace of God it will continue to be your condition *for all eternity*, and justly so. God has said that what sin deserves is death—separation from God. And we have sinned and are under that sentence now—without God and without hope in the world. That is our problem.

The death of Jesus in our place is our only hope. It is the only answer because it is God's answer. The Word of God says two things: 'The wages of sin is death' (Romans 6:23) and 'Without the shedding of blood there is no forgiveness' (Hebrews 9:22). These pronouncements are the just declarations of the holy God, and they can never be abolished or by-passed. On the cross, dying at the wish of his Father (because God in his mercy planned to save sinners), Jesus satisfies these demands. He does this by dying in the sinner's place—by what our forefathers have called his work of 'substitution' and 'propitiation'.

Substitution

Consider carefully the following statements:

> The Lord has laid on him the iniquity of us all (Isaiah 53:6).
> He himself bore our sins in his body on the tree (1 Peter 2:24).
> God made him who had no sin to be sin for us (2 Corinthians 5:21).

Each of them tells us that Jesus died *in our place*. We deserve to die, but he died instead of us. He became our substitute. To use an Old Testament illustration, he became the 'scapegoat' (Leviticus 16)—the innocent victim bearing the guilt of others and suffering their just punishment. This was God's plan to make salvation possible for guilty sinners.

Propitiation

The Authorized Version of Romans 3:25 reads, 'whom God hath set forth to be a propitiation through faith in his blood'. This word 'propitiation', however, is not found in modern translations of the Bible. Instead, the New International Version uses the phrase 'sacrifice of atonement'. What it means is that on the cross Jesus, bearing our sin and guilt, faced the wrath of God instead of us and paid fully on our behalf the debt we owed to the broken law of God. On the cross our Savior cried, 'My God, my God, why have you forsaken me?' (Matthew 27:46). The holy God forsook his Son because he was our sin-bearer. 'God made him who had no sin to be sin for us' (2 Corinthians 5:21). Jesus was 'stricken by God, smitten by him, and afflicted' (Isaiah 53:4). The Old Testament prophecy of Zechariah 13:7 was being fulfilled: 'Awake, O sword, against my shepherd...declares the Lord Almighty. Strike the shepherd...' The sword was the sword of judgment, and in Matthew 26:31 Jesus tells us clearly that this verse speaks of him. This is how the hymn-writer puts it:

> Jehovah lifted up His rod:
> O Christ, it fell on Thee!
> Thou wast sore stricken of Thy God;
> There's not one stroke for me.
> Thy tears, Thy blood, beneath it flowed;
> Thy bruising healeth me.

> Jehovah bade His sword awake:
>   O Christ, it woke 'gainst Thee;
> Thy blood the flaming blade must slake,
>   Thy heart its sheath must be.
> All for my sake, my peace to make:
>   Now sleeps that sword for me.

At Calvary, in other words, our Lord made it possible for a holy God to be propitious—or favorably inclined—toward us even though we were sinners and had broken his holy law. God dealt with the problem of sin in the only way that could satisfy his holy justice and enable him to move in and break the power of Satan in sinners' lives. To think that our efforts could do this is totally to devalue the holiness of God and seriously to underestimate the terribleness of sin in God's sight. We are redeemed, set free from sin's bondage, 'not with perishable things such as silver or gold ...but with the precious blood of Christ, a lamb without blemish or defect' (1 Peter 1:18, 19).

The resurrection of Jesus confirms for us that his atoning death was God's plan. It also assures us that the holy God has accepted the atonement made by our Lord on behalf of sinners. Jesus was 'declared with power to be the Son of God by his resurrection from the dead' (Romans 1:4). 'He was delivered over to death for our sins and was raised to life for our justification' (Romans 4:25). 'Death has been swallowed up in victory. Where, O death, is your victory? Where, O death, is your sting? The sting of death is sin, and the power of sin is the law. But thanks be to God! He gives us the victory through our Lord Jesus Christ' (1 Corinthians 15:54-57).

It was the holiness of God that made the atonement necessary, but it was the love of God that made it possible. If God had not loved us, then he would never have sent his Son to die for us.

> From whence this fear and unbelief?
> Hath not the Father put to grief
>   His spotless Son for me?
> And will the righteous Judge of men
> Condemn me for that debt of sin
>   Which, Lord, was charged on Thee?

Complete atonement Thou hast made,
And to the utmost Thou hast paid
   Whate'er Thy people owed;
How then can wrath on me take place,
If sheltered in Thy righteousness,
   And sprinkled with Thy blood?

It is finished

On the cross Jesus uttered the remarkable words: 'It is finished' (John 19:30). He did not mean that his life was finished. He was referring to God's plan of salvation. The problem of sin had been dealt with. Jesus had once and for all 'offered for all time one sacrifice for sins' (Hebrews 10:12).

The story is told of a Christian farmer who was very concerned about a friend of his who was unsaved. On many occasions the farmer had explained to his friend the gospel of God's grace, and how the finished work of Christ was a sufficient sacrifice for the salvation of his soul. But the friend, a carpenter, would not accept this, and insisted that if his soul were to be saved he himself had to contribute something to that end. One day the farmer asked the carpenter to make a gate for him. The work was done, the gate was collected, and the carpenter was to meet the farmer the next day to fit the finished work in its appointed place. When he arrived, he was surprised to find the farmer waiting for him with a sharp axe in his hand. 'What is that for?' he asked. 'I am going to add improvements to your work', said the carpenter. 'But there's no need for that,' said the carpenter. 'The gate is perfectly all right. I have done all that was necessary.' Ignoring his friend, the farmer began chipping away with the axe until the gate was spoiled. 'Look what you have done!' cried the carpenter, 'You have ruined my work!' 'Yes', replied the Christian farmer, 'and that is exactly what you are trying to do to the finished work of the Lord Jesus Christ with your own miserable efforts.'

Reader, *'It is finished'!* Jesus has done all that is necessary for your salvation. Do not try to add to it. There is no need.

6. The Work of the Spirit

If you have read as far as this, you have been learning from the Scriptures, perhaps for the first time, what you are really like in the sight of God, and what God has done about it. What is your reaction so far to what you have read?

Anger

Perhaps it has made you angry. You do not like it one bit. You resent being told that you are a sinner. But listen: 'If we claim to be without sin, we deceive ourselves and the truth is not in us' (1 John 1:8). Perhaps you particularly resent being told that you can do nothing about it. But if we could save ourselves, if there was any other way, do you think that God would have let Jesus suffer the humiliation and agony of the cross?

But that is not all. The truth of the matter is that man, apart from God's intervention in his life, does not wish to be changed. 'There is ...no one who seeks God ...the sinful mind is hostile to God' (Romans 3:11; 8:7). God's problem, if he was to save man, was twofold. He himself had to provide someone who could take the penalty which man deserves because of his sin—and that, as we have seen, happened at Calvary. But there still remained the other problem of man's unwillingness to turn to God and take advantage of God's readiness to receive him and pardon his sins through Jesus Christ. And sometimes men are not just unwilling, but plain angry at being told that they need to turn to God at all, or to thank Jesus Christ for what he did on the cross for the sake of unworthy, guilty sinners.

Confusion

It may be that the teaching of this book is different from that which you have been told or taught to believe in the past. You therefore feel somewhat confused and bewildered. I would urge you to follow the example of the Bereans in Acts 17:11. They 'examined the Scriptures every day to see if what Paul said was true'. I would urge you also to ask God to enlighten you, just in case what you are reading and what you will see in the Scriptures may be true.

19

Fear

On the other hand, you may be one who has no doubt as to the truth of what you are reading. You realize your perilous condition before God and it has caused you to fear. You want to be saved. You want to know God. Perhaps you have even asked God to forgive you, but nothing seems to have happened. And so you begin to despair. Fear is not a bad initial reaction to the gospel, but do not despair. Read on.

The work of the Holy Spirit

It is possible to hear the gospel many times and never be concerned about it. The following experience is not unusual: 'I had been attending church for years, but I had never really listened to what was being preached. Then for some unknown reason the preaching began to disturb me, until one Sunday I felt that the preacher was speaking only about me. I felt as if every eye in the church was upon me. I wanted to run away and hide.'

The explanation for that is not that the preaching suddenly improved, but that the Holy Spirit had begun to speak through the preached gospel to the heart and conscience of the sinner. We have seen that we cannot save ourselves; but neither can any preacher or church save us. Salvation is the work of God. It is his exclusive work. It has to be, because of what we are by nature. Jesus said that we must be born again of the Holy Spirit because only 'the Spirit gives birth to spirit' (John 3:6)—that is, to a new spirit that is willing to serve God. Only the Holy Spirit can produce a spiritual change in man. Many other agencies can change an individual—some for the better, some for the worse. A person may discover the joys of music and this may greatly enrich his life; or his life may be ruined by alcohol. But none of these changes affects what that man is before a holy God. He is born a sinner, and whether his life is enriched by music or ruined by alcohol, he remains a sinner—a cultured sinner or a drunken sinner, but still a sinner. To alter a man's standing before God, a spiritual change is needed. This is the work of the Holy Spirit, and Jesus calls the beginning of this change being 'born again'. And he means what he says. You need to be born again—nothing else will do.

Your problem is that you, like everyone else, were born a sinner. Therefore you need a new birth which will replace your sinful nature with a spiritual nature that knows and loves God. To be born again is an outstanding experience. It is God working a change in your heart which influences every part of your life, so that you are a new person. It is the first work of God in a soul, and it is the forerunner of faith and repentance.

Conviction of sin

The first work of the Holy Spirit of which the sinner himself is aware is commonly called 'conviction of sin'. This means that a man is given a very real awareness of his own guilt and condemnation before a holy and righteous God. There may be different degrees of conviction, for some feel their guilt more intensely than others. The period of conviction can vary also, lasting a matter of hours, days or even months. Again, the Holy Spirit can use various means to bring about this conviction of one's sinfulness and guilt. The primary means has always been through the preaching of the gospel, as in Acts 2:14-37; but it can happen through God's control of circumstances, as with the Prodigal Son in Luke 15:11-24, or sometimes through observing the life of someone who is a Christian, or indeed in many other ways. What matters, however, is that we are convicted of the truth about ourselves in relation to God.

Conviction is essential to salvation, because unless you know you are a condemned sinner you will never seek the Savior. You may hear the gospel a hundred times over, but without conviction of sin it will never be 'good news' to you because you will see no need of it.

Imagine yourself on a warm summer afternoon sitting in a deck-chair at a seaside resort enjoying an ice cream. Someone tells you that at that resort they have the finest lifeguards in the country. You do not doubt the truth of the statement, but neither does the statement excite your heart. After all, who needs a lifeguard while sitting comfortably in a deck-chair? But now imagine yourself at that same resort, except that instead of being in a deck-chair you are half a mile out to sea, and you have cramps and are beginning to drown. Suddenly, you remember what you have heard about those wonderful lifeguards, and that same truth to which before you were quite indifferent is now a matter of life and death. You shout for help, knowing that without the life-guards you are doomed. What is it that has changed? Not the truth itself, but your appreciation of it, and this has been brought about by an awareness of your need.

Conviction of sin changes a person's attitude toward the gospel. Do you know that you are a sinner? Do you realize that God is angry with you, and that you are going to hell? You have only one hope, and that is in the gospel of the Lord Jesus Christ. 'Salvation is found in no one else, for there is no other name under heaven given to men by which we must be saved' (Acts 4:12).

Jesus said that the Holy Spirit 'will convict the world of guilt in regard to sin and righteousness and judgment: in regard to sin, because men do not believe in me; in regard to righteousness, because I am going to the Father where you can see me no longer; and in regard to judgment, because the prince of this world now stands condemned' (John 16:8-11).

Has the Holy Spirit convicted you of these things? Are you convicted with regard to your sin—and particularly the greatest sin of all, the sin of unbelief? Has he begun to show you the righteousness and beauty of Jesus? Have you been made aware of the coming judgment, not only of Satan, the prince of this world, but of all who, like that Evil One, reject God's authority?

If not, ask God to bring conviction to you. It is not a very pleasant experience, but it is absolutely necessary. All who have come to God have come this way, and it is only those who have known conviction of sin who have gone on to know peace with God, an assurance that their sins are forgiven, and a full satisfaction of all their needs in the Lord Jesus Christ. As has been said earlier, the degree of conviction and the period it lasts may vary from one person to another: with some it can be long, intense and agonizing; with others, swift and momentary. Do not make the mistake of judging the reality of your experience by comparing it with someone else's. The important question is: *Do you know you are a sinner, and are you aware of the consequences?* If so, then, like those convicted of sins in Acts 2:37, you are beginning to ask, 'What shall I do?' The answer which those people were given is still the same for you: 'Repent!'

7. REPENTANCE AND FAITH

Repentance

Repentance is not a case of you trying your best to put right all the sin there is in your life. Repentance means that the sinner, conscious of his guilt, and aware of the mercy of God in Christ, turns from his sin to God. The repentant sinner knows a loathing and a hatred of sin and a great desire to live in obedience to God. He will cry to God for mercy and pardon.

There is no salvation without repentance. When Jesus began preaching, his first words were: 'Repent, for the kingdom of heaven is near' (Matthew 4:17). The Scriptures tell us that God now 'commands all people everywhere to repent' (Acts 17:30).

Repentance means more than being sorry for your sins. It is possible to be sorry for the trouble and distress that sin has caused you without giving the slightest thought to what your sin has done to God. All sin is against God. It robs him of honor and glory. The truly repentant sinner grieves more over this aspect of it than anything else. He has sinned against God and he knows it. The work of the Holy Spirit in the sinner causes a change in his entire attitude toward God and his claims on his life. Sin is seen for what it really is: not just a character defect, but a permanent state of rebellion against the love and care and righteous authority of a holy God. It is this new understanding of God and one's own sin that leads to repentance. There will be a great desire to break with the past and to live from now on only to please God and for his glory. That is repentance.

Faith

Accompanying repentance there is always faith. Faith enables us to believe not only in the existence of God, but in the love of God and the full pardon which he offers in the Lord Jesus Christ. In order to have faith in Jesus Christ you must obviously have first been made aware of the gospel. You will have heard and in a measure understood its teaching. More than that, you will have come in a very real sense to believe it. All this takes place in your mind, and there can be no faith without it.

But this is not enough to save your soul. Saving faith progresses from an intellectual acceptance of certain facts to a real trusting in Christ and in what he has done on your behalf and for your salvation. Faith is a response of the heart and the mind to the Savior of whom the gospel has told you.

Faith is not blind. It is not a step in the dark. It rests on the very solid foundation of the person of Jesus Christ. In faith you believe:

- that the Lord Jesus Christ is God—'the Word was God ...the Word became flesh' (John 1:1,14).
- that he died for your sin—he came 'to give his life as a ransom for many' (Matthew 20:28); 'Christ ...who loved me and gave himself for me' (Galatians 2:20).
- that he is the only Savior—'I am the way and the truth and the life. No one comes to the Father except through me' (John 14:6).
- that he is willing to save you—'Come to me, all you who are weary and burdened, and I will give you rest' (Matthew 11:28).
- that without him you have no hope—'And this is the testimony: God has given us eternal life, and this life is in his Son. He who has the Son has life; he who does not have the Son of God does not have life' (1 John 5:11, 12).

Believing these truths, you come to God in repentance, 'being fully persuaded that God [has] power to do what he [has] promised' (Romans 4:21), and with faith in the Lord Jesus Christ you ask God to pardon your sin and cleanse you in the precious blood of the Savior. You do this, believing the promise that 'To all who received him, to those who believed in his name, he gave the right to become children of God—children born not of natural descent, nor of human decision or a husband's will, but born of God' (John 1:12, 13).

8. ACCEPTANCE BY GOD

When a sinner comes to God in faith and repentance, he does so not simply because of an act of his will. There is always an earlier work of the Holy Spirit. He comes because God is drawing him. Jesus said, 'No one can come to me unless the Father who sent me draws him' (John 6:44). This really is a most thrilling truth. Just think of it—God drawing you to himself, the Holy Spirit working personally on your heart to bring you to God! God does this because he loved you long before you ever thought about him: 'This is love: not that we loved God, but that he loved us and sent his Son as an atoning sacrifice for our sins' (1 John 4:10). Salvation originates in God, not with us. Thank God that it does, or we would never be saved.

When you come to God on his terms—in faith and repentance—it is because he loves you and has drawn you to him. He then freely and unreservedly forgives you all your sin, past, present and future: 'For I will forgive their wickedness and will remember their sins no more' (Jeremiah 31:34); 'as far as the east is from the west, so far has he removed our transgressions from us' (Psalm 103:12). Instead of your being God's enemy, he makes you his child. You are accepted because of the Lord Jesus Christ: 'In him [Jesus] we have redemption through his blood, the forgiveness of sins' (Ephesians 1:7).

This in itself is tremendous, but salvation and acceptance by God include much more.

A new righteousness—in Christ

In salvation God credits us with the righteousness of Jesus. He sees us hidden in the Savior and covered with the holy, sinless character of Christ. 'For he has clothed me with garments of salvation and arrayed me

25

in a robe of righteousness' (Isaiah 61:10). It is this alone that makes guilty, vile sinners acceptable to God. And this righteousness is available only through Jesus: 'This righteousness from God comes through faith in Jesus Christ to all who believe' (Romans 3:22).

The Bible calls this *justification*. It restores to us what we lost through sin—peace with God and access to him. 'Therefore, since we have been justified through faith, we have peace with God through our Lord Jesus Christ, through whom we have gained access by faith into this grace in which we now stand' (Romans 5:1,2).

A new nature—by the Spirit

God will not just forgive you and urge you to be better in the future. The fact is that you could not be better because of your sinful nature. God knows this, so when you come to him in repentance and faith he gives you a new nature. 'I will give you a new heart and put a new spirit in you; I will remove from you your heart of stone and give you a heart of flesh. And I will put my Spirit in you and move you to follow my decrees and be careful to keep my laws' (Ezekiel 36:26, 27).

The Bible calls this *sanctification*. It is the new righteousness we have in Christ flowing through our life, governing our actions and being seen in our daily living.

Salvation is no small thing. It is an act of outstanding significance: 'If anyone is in Christ, he is a new creation; the old has gone, the new has come!' (2 Corinthians 5:17). This new nature means that the law of God, which previously went very much against the grain, is now for you the only way to live. You will fail on many occasions to live up to God's standard, but the new nature keeps you going in the right direction.

A new relationship—to the Father

We sometimes read of a king or a president issuing a pardon to criminals in prison. But we never go on to read of the king waiting outside the prison to embrace the released prisoner and insisting he come home to

26

the palace to be treated from then on as a child of the king. Yet that is exactly what God does for us! Salvation means that 'You are no longer foreigners and aliens, but fellow-citizens with God's people and members of God's household' (Ephesians 2:19).

The Bible calls this *adoption*: 'Those who are led by the Spirit of God are sons of God. For ...you received the Spirit of sonship. And by him we cry, "*Abba*, Father"' (Romans 8:14,15). The truth is that we *belong* to God. Little wonder that the Bible calls it '*so great salvation*'!

There are many who, immediately before conversion, ask , 'Will I be able to keep it up? Will I be able to live the new life?' The answer is that God not only saves, but he keeps. The new righteousness, the new nature, and the new relationship that come to the sinner in salvation are blessings that cannot be imagined beforehand. But this is what salvation is. It is more than forgiveness: with forgiveness and pardon come new life in Christ. Jesus said, 'I give them eternal life, and they shall never perish; no one can snatch them out of my hand. My Father, who has given them to me, is greater than all; no one can snatch them out of my Father's hand' (John 10:28,29).

9. COME!

In your search for God, are you beginning to despair of ever finding him? Here is a great encouragement for you: it is not so much that you are seeking God, but that God is seeking you. Jesus came into this world 'to seek and to save what was lost' (Luke 19:10).

In Luke 15, Jesus tells three parables—of the Lost Sheep, the Lost Coin, and the Lost Son. Read the chapter, and notice at the end of each parable the great rejoicing when the lost is found. Jesus tells us also that 'There is rejoicing in the presence of the angels of God over one sinner who repents' (verse 10). Are you beginning to see now how much value God places on the souls of men and women like you? Your search for God is not a hopeless one, for he has promised, 'You will seek me and find me when you seek me with all your heart. I will be found by you ...'

(Jeremiah 29:13,14). This is the gospel, the 'good news': 'God so loved the world that he gave his one and only Son, that whoever believes in him shall not perish but have eternal life' (John 3:16). If you have read the pages of this little book with any understanding, you cannot doubt his love. There remains but one word from the gospel to bring to you. It is a small word, a simple word, but it is of vital importance. The word is 'Come!' Jesus said, 'Come to me, all you who are weary and burdened, and I will give you rest ...rest for your souls' (Matthew 11:28, 29). Are you weary and burdened with the load and guilt of your sin? Then come to Christ! You want rest for your soul, don't you? Then come!

Jesus said, 'Come, for everything is now ready' (Luke 14:17). There is nothing you have to do, neither is there anything that God has to do, for Jesus has already done all that is necessary for your salvation. 'It is finished', it is ready; so come!

Almost the last words in the Bible are: 'Whoever is thirsty, let him come; and whoever wishes, let him take the free gift of the water of life' (Revelation 22:17). A great preacher speaking on this verse once said:

> My text is such a precious one, that I cannot enter into the fulness of its freeness and sweetness. Remember, my dear friends, if you are willing to be saved, God requires nothing of you except that you will yield yourselves up to Christ. If you are willing to be saved, none can prevent, there is no obstacle. You are come where Jesus stands—stands with open arms, stands with open mouth, crying to you this day, 'If any man thirst, let him come unto me, and drink ...And whosoever will, let him take the water of life freely.'
>
> And now will you refuse the invitation? Will you go this day and abuse the free mercy of God? Shall his very mercy lead you into more sin? Will you be wicked enough to say, that because grace is free, therefore you will continue in sin year after year? Oh, do not do so; grieve not the Spirit of God: today is the accepted time; today is the day of salvation.

To 'come' means to believe in Jesus, to trust him, commit your soul to him and be saved. This is beautifully illustrated in the parable of the Lost Son in Luke 15. Read carefully from verse 17 to verse 24. The words 'He came to his senses' mean that he began to think seriously about what had happened. We see him reviewing his life. He has stopped thinking super-ficially, and for the first time he is seeing things as they really are. What a mess he is in! How desperate his need is! Are you in this situation?

He realizes that there is only one answer: he must go back to his father. Why? Because he has come to the conclusion that the decision to leave home was not just a bad mistake; it was sin—sin against his father and sin against heaven, that is, against God. His sin has caused him great misery, but, more than that, it has caused misery both to his father and to God. Is this how you are thinking at the moment? Then do something about it. In verses 17-19 we see the Lost Son deciding on the right course to take, and then in verse 20 he acts upon it.

It may be that by the grace of God you can clearly see the problem of sin and you now know the way of salvation. Do not stop at that: come to God! Once you make that response to God of repentance and faith, you will realize that God the Father is moving toward you in love and compassion, just as the Lost Son did. There will be no need to ask, 'Will he receive me?' God loves you, Jesus died for you, the Holy Spirit is drawing you, so come! Read again verses 20-24 and see there the wonderful reception a repentant sinner receives from God himself.

Come to God like this, and your seeking will be over. You will have found God; you will have found salvation and peace in the Lord Jesus Christ forever!

◆◆◆◆◆◆◆◆◆◆◆◆

If you desire help in your journey, the publishers of this little book would like to help you locate a church that teaches the Word of God faithfully. Contact us:

BRYNTIRION Press
c/o Evangelical Press (UK)
    e-mail: sales@evangelicalpress.org
    write: Faverdale North, Darlington DL3 OPH England
Solid Ground Christian Books (USA)
    e-mail: solid_ground_books@yahoo.com
    write: PO Box 660132, Vestavia Hills, AL 35266

Other Peter Jeffery titles for further study

Christian Handbook, BRYNTIRION Press
ISBN: 1 85049 065 1
—This is a simple, straightforward guide to the Bible, church history and Christian doctrine.

Opening Up Ephesians, Solid Ground Books and Evangelical Press
ISBN: 0 9710169 7 6
—This is a pointed and practical explanation of Paul's Epistle to the Ephesians especially intended for those beginning the Christian life.

Bitesize Theology, Evangelical Press
ISBN: 0 85234 447 3
—In this easy-to-read book, Peter Jeffery shows us how tantalizingly enjoyable Bible teaching can be. With short but solid chapters on key subjects, he outlines the ABC's of the Christian faith.